Go Girl
WIN!

# Go Girl
# WIN!

## Crystal D. Freeman

purposely
created
PUBLISHING

**GO GIRL, WIN**
Published by Purposely Created Publishing Group™

Copyright © 2019 Crystal D. Freeman

Printed in the United States of America

ISBN: 978-1-949134-85-8

Special discounts are available on bulk quantity purchases by book clubs, associations and special interest groups. For details email: sales@publishyourgift.com or call (888) 949-6228.

For information log on to www.PublishYourGift.com

I dedicate this book to my beautiful daughter, Heavenly. You have birthed the winner within me. You have given me a reason to strive. From this day forward, I prayer you hold fast to every word in this book. Some days may seem challenging, but remember *GO GIRL, WIN*!!!

Love,
Mom

# Table of Contents

# Introduction

What you are holding in your hands is not just another book with cute words strung together to make you feel good for a moment. No, these words have been carefully crafted to empower you for a lifetime. My hope is that you will appreciate my kick in the pants because I am your sister and I refuse to let you fail.

The truth is these affirmations will sometimes be challenging to declare, but I encourage you to speak them until you believe them. If you have to, stand in front of the mirror and repeat them over and over until the words are so buried in your heart that neither the opinions of others nor the storms of life will be able to uproot them. These life-changing affirmations were written to help you reside in a place of confidence and achieve success on your own terms. So, use this book daily to remind yourself of your power. Feel free to read these affirmations as many times as you need to. Let them sink in. Keep this book with you, declare these words when you need a dose of encouragement, and journal your thoughts to heal your soul and manifest your goals. Each affirmation is followed by a motivational prompt that will help you to spark immediate action and secure your win.

As you make these declarations personal, I hope you will be invigorated to boldly live your life to the fullest; no holds barred. Don't back down. Don't throw in the towel. Don't give up. Instead, elevate your mindset, stand in your power, and rise to your greatest potential. And when you encounter other women who need to be reminded of their greatness, I hope you will tell them *GO GIRL, WIN*!

# Thirteen Steps to Being Successful at What You Do

:

1.

Keep God first.

**2.**

Be passionate about what
you're trying to achieve.

# 3.

## Focus on every opportunity.

4.

Work hard. Success only comes from hard work.

5.

Enjoy the journey because
the road to success is
very long.

6.

Never stop learning.

**7.**

Never feel like you

have arrived.

8.

Trust your gut instinct more
than anyone's opinion.

9.

Be persistent.

10.

Rely on your team.

11.

Be honest and show
integrity.

**12.**

**Appreciate your success by giving back.**

13.

Pray to God for a successor
that you may mentor.

50 Affirmations to

Help You Win

**The only thing you should fear is living but not reaching your full potential. Everyone is born with a purpose.**

My purpose on this earth is...

_____

_____

_____

_____

_____

_____

_____

_____

**Stay busy improving yourself so that you don't have time to pay attention to anything or anyone that distracts you from growth.**

What 3 areas of your life do you need to focus on improving?

_____

_____

_____

_____

_____

_____

_____

_____

**Sometimes you must celebrate yourself. Even if it's something small, be proud of yourself. Become your biggest supporter.**

Celebrate a recent accomplishment.

_____

_____

_____

_____

_____

_____

_____

**Stop having friends who don't tell you when you aren't living up to your potential. Be around people who tell you when you're wrong and stick around to watch you get it right. That's a real friend.**

List 5 people in your life who fit this description of a real friend.

_____

_____

_____

_____

_____

_____

_____

_____

**Don't let anyone interrupt your greatness. Some people just need to admire you from afar. Everyone isn't meant to be a part of your life.**

List 5 people you need to distance yourself from as soon as possible.

_____

_____

_____

_____

_____

_____

_____

**No boy on this earth will ever be cute enough to distract you from getting an education.**

❮❮❮❮❮

Who is distracting you? What boundaries can you set to keep that from happening?

_____

_____

_____

_____

_____

_____

_____

_____

**When you see another woman winning that doesn't mean you're losing, it simply means anything is possible.**

Who is your shero? What tips of hers can you incorporate into your own life to help you win?

_____

_____

_____

_____

_____

_____

_____

**Choose the person you desire to become over everything. Sometimes focusing on yourself will cost you relationships and material things.**

~~~∞~~~

Who do you desire to become? What steps can you start taking today to become that person?

_____

_____

_____

_____

_____

_____

_____

_____

**Sometimes to find out who you are you have to be hurt by the ones you love the most. Sometimes you will lose people to find your true identity.**

What loss made you better?

_____

_____

_____

_____

_____

_____

_____

_____

**Never let something or someone that has nothing to do with your future distract you. Stay focused on the journey ahead.**

List 3 things you want to achieve within the next 3 months.

_____

_____

_____

_____

_____

_____

_____

_____

**Today, know who you are, know what you want, and don't settle for less.**

What are 5 powerful words that describe you?

_____

_____

_____

_____

_____

_____

_____

_____

We live in a society that calls being smart dumb, but never fear being the intelligent person in the room. Remember that being beautiful has nothing to do with the mind. I have met several people who are beautiful but have no sense of direction. Educate your mind.

What was the last book you read to help expand your mind?

_____

_____

_____

_____

_____

_____

_____

_____

**To the woman who has become depressed because of how society says you should look. Girl, you are beautiful with all your flaws. Don't allow society to put you in a box. Be free, Girl.**

———∞———

In what areas of your life have you given yourself permission to be free?

_____

_____

_____

_____

_____

_____

_____

**When you truly don't care about what anyone thinks of you and you are not out here trying to impress everyone that's when you start winning.**

⌇∞⌇

Who do you need to stop trying to impress?

_____

_____

_____

_____

_____

_____

_____

_____

## Winning Affirmation 15

**A lot of people will become pissed off when they see you winning. That's ok. You weren't born to get everyone's approval. Live your life, Girl.**

How are you living your life despite your haters?

_____

_____

_____

_____

_____

_____

_____

_____

**Never be ashamed to start from the bottom. It's ok for people to see you struggle. Those same people will become your cheerleaders later when you're winning. There's no shame in working hard to become successful.**

What sacrifices have you had to make to become successful? Remind yourself that they are worth it.

_____

_____

_____

_____

_____

_____

_____

_____

**Choose today to protect your peace
on every level. Avoid toxic people to
protect yourself mentally and spiritually.
Only you have the power to turn away
negative energy.**

List 3 things you can do to protect
your peace.

_____

_____

_____

_____

_____

_____

_____

_____

One day you will realize you're too grown to worry about who likes or dislikes you. You should live like this: if you love me, I love you. If you support me, I support you. But, if you hate me, that's your problem. Life goes on with or without you.

⎯⎯⎯∞⎯⎯⎯

Vow to keep living no matter what.

_____

_____

_____

_____

_____

_____

_____

## Winning Affirmation 19

## Eight Daily Reminders:

1. I am beautiful.

2. I can do anything.

3. Positivity is a choice.

4. I will celebrate my individuality.

5. I am prepared for success.

6. I am loved.

7. I am amazing.

8. I won't fail.

Remind yourself of these truths daily.

**Never let anyone rush your process to success. We all develop differently. The goal is to never stop evolving, never stop believing, and never stop praying for the better you.**

Draw a picture of a butterfly. Let it remind you that you've come a long way. Remember it had to evolve too.

**Today, go in with this mentality: I will make this happen. My past will not hold me down. My present situation will get better. I am an overcomer!**

~⦾∞⦿~

Write this affirmation down. Seeing it will help you to believe it.

_____

_____

_____

_____

_____

_____

_____

_____

**When you begin to erase unnecessary drama and problems from your life, the right things will begin to fall into place. Sometimes you have to let go of things in your life that don't serve a positive purpose.**

What negative person or thing do you need to release in order to receive?

_____

_____

_____

_____

_____

_____

_____

_____

## Eight Things You Need to Focus on Today:

1. Focus on your purpose.

2. Focus on your physical strength.

3. Focus on your mental wellness.

4. Focus on having more fun.

5. Focus on being less stressed.

6. Focus on simplifying your life.

7. Focus on your real friends.

8. Focus on truly living your life.

Add "I will" before these and speak them aloud.

Today, walk with your head up and remain confident yet humble. Someone will always try to do what you're doing. Whatever your purpose, God has gifted you to do it. There's enough room for everyone to win!!!

List at least 3 things that make you unique.

_____

_____

_____

_____

_____

_____

_____

_____

**Don't be afraid of change. Sometimes change means leaving a job or cutting off toxic people. You must continue to become a better version of yourself.**

Make a pros and cons list of the things you have been wanting to change, then go for it.

_____

_____

_____

_____

_____

_____

_____

_____

**Nothing in life will ever go exactly as planned. Sometimes it's ok to plan for failure and winning at the same time. That's a part of the conditioning process of life.**

When did an unexpected detour turn out to be for your good?

_____

_____

_____

_____

_____

_____

_____

_____

**The truth is that sometimes people will possess more than you yet still be jealous of you simply because you know who you are and your confidence brightens up a room.**

What do others think are your best qualities?

_____

_____

_____

_____

_____

_____

_____

_____

**Sometimes you must have your own back. You must be your biggest fan, knowing that one day all this hard work will pay off.**

Write yourself a note explaining why you are your biggest fan.

_____

_____

_____

_____

_____

_____

_____

_____

**Never settle for being the girl society said you should become. Be the girl who loves herself whether she is wearing a size six or fourteen. Confidence is self-esteem that can never be overlooked.**

Put on your favorite dress and slay.

_____

_____

_____

_____

_____

_____

_____

_____

**Continue to evolve every day so that you don't have time to pay attention to anyone else's life. Someone else's business is a complete distraction from your own life.**

What goals do you need to focus on achieving?

_____

_____

_____

_____

_____

_____

_____

_____

**As you begin to grow deeper in your own craft, never be the type of woman who tries to step over another woman's success. It's ok to tell someone who does the same exact things you do that they're doing a good job.**

What woman can you give a compliment to today?

_____

_____

_____

_____

_____

_____

_____

_____

**When you become confident in who you are you will attract success. Your value will increase and the right people will begin to track you down. The beauty of your confidence starts from within.**

In what areas of your life do you display the most confidence?

_____

_____

_____

_____

_____

_____

_____

_____

**Eventually you will stop being around people who always have the latest gossip and hang around people who always have the latest business move. That's when you go from being a girl to being a woman.**

Find an accountability partner that will help you get to the next level.

_____

_____

_____

_____

_____

_____

_____

**Success doesn't come because of how you feel. You can't just do good when you feel good. You have to do good even when you feel bad. Eventually it will be worth it.**

What is your definition of success? Write it here so that you know what to aspire to even on your bad days.

_____

_____

_____

_____

_____

_____

_____

_____

**Let them think whatever they want
to about you. People assume every day,
you just keep getting better
by the minute.**

~eᴄᴄᴄᴇ~

Decide today to stop giving power to
other people's opinions.

_____

_____

_____

_____

_____

_____

_____

_____

**You can't knock a woman out of a position God gave her. Stop allowing people to tell you that you need them to win when God created you with purpose.**

~~~∞~~~

Read Jeremiah 29:11 and journal your thoughts.

_____

_____

_____

_____

_____

_____

_____

_____

**Be selfish with the person you're becoming. In order to become the best you, you might have to change some friendships.**

What friends do you have to remove from your circle?

_____

_____

_____

_____

_____

_____

_____

_____

**Never give people authority over your
dreams and goals. Only you have the
power to determine what will happen
in your life.**

~~~∞∞~~~

What step can you make today to take
back your power?

_____

_____

_____

_____

_____

_____

_____

_____

**You must tell yourself: "Today is the last day fear or doubt will enter my mind. I will win, I am victorious, I am built for this day."**

～ﾟ∞ﾟ～

Go ahead, tell yourself.

_____

_____

_____

_____

_____

_____

_____

**Nobody owes you anything. Make yourself a promise to become better every day. Love yourself, forgive people, and keep a positive mindset.**

What promises do you need to make to yourself? Write them down, then keep them.

_____

_____

_____

_____

_____

_____

_____

_____

**Never try to force people or things to stay in your life. Someone who loves you will never have to question their love or loyalty. Don't force life, live it.**

Today I choose to release:

_____

_____

_____

_____

_____

_____

_____

_____

**Sometimes being successful means pain, long days, and long nights. But, in the end, success can be sweet. Stay focused. A sweet future is ahead.**

What sweet successes have you had lately?

_____

_____

_____

_____

_____

_____

_____

_____

## Nine Ways to Stay Motivated:

1. Take it one day at a time.

2. Support yourself by being positive.

3. Make achievable goals.

4. Reward yourself.

5. Believe in yourself.

6. Acknowledge your positive attributes.

7. Recognize your progress.

8. Visualize accomplishing your goals.

9. Be kind to yourself.

Make it a point to do at least one
of these every day.

## Winning Affirmation 44

**Smile more. Be excited. Throw away
your clutter. Unfollow negative people
on social media. Don't gossip. Do things
that challenge you.**

Put on your favorite lipstick and smile big.

_____

_____

_____

_____

_____

_____

_____

_____

**There was a time when you were a little girl with big dreams and you promised yourself you'd make them real one day. Don't disappoint the little girl within.**

What are 5 dreams you still need to accomplish?

_____

_____

_____

_____

_____

_____

_____

**You are not your past. You are not your pain. You are not the lies spoken against you. You were born a little girl with big dreams, conquer them one day at a time. You will win.**

Vow today to stop reliving your past pains.

_____

_____

_____

_____

_____

_____

_____

_____

**You're never too old to dream and you're never too young to develop your dreams. *GO GIRL, WIN!***

What steps can you take today to help you develop your dreams?

_____

_____

_____

_____

_____

_____

_____

**Everything you're going through today is preparing you for your tomorrow. Stay positive and continue to grow. Conquer every fear. You will win.**

What is 1 major fear you can face head on today?

_____

_____

_____

_____

_____

_____

_____

_____

**Stop apologizing to people who hate your success. Accept that you are a winner. You deserve to laugh, you deserve your peace, you are unique. They have to accept the fact that you are unstoppable.**

Brag about yourself today to a friend, a co-worker, or all of your followers on social media.

_____

_____

_____

_____

_____

_____

_____

_____

**Never run after people to prove that you matter. Love yourself. The right people will come to admire your beautiful character. You are loved.**

List 10 people who love and support you.

_____

_____

_____

_____

_____

_____

_____

_____

_____

_____

# Seven Rules for Self-Love

1.

Let go of what is
hurting you.

**2.**

Don't be afraid to say no.

3.

Never try to please people.

4.

Trust your instincts.

5.

Love yourself.

**6.**

Never speak badly about
yourself.

7.

If it feels wrong
don't do it.

# About the Author

Crystal Freeman is a mother, author, entrepreneur, and encourager. Her passion is to help young women understand and actualize their purpose. Crystal has received a Women of Excellence award from the Women of Pearls Organization. She has also been recognized by various organizations throughout her community for her contributions to others and love for kids. In 2016, Crystal launched the Women of the Overcomer gathering. She is also the founder of the Global Overcomers Foundation, and author of *Memoirs of an Overcomer* and *Inspirations of an Overcomer*.

In her spare time, Crystal enjoys fishing, swimming, and playing board games with her children. She is the proud mother of Jailen and Heavenly.

To connect, visit her website a
www.msovercomer.com

www.ingramcontent.com/pod-product-compliance
Lightning Source LLC
Chambersburg PA
CBHW071502210326
41597CB00018B/2655